Czarist Russia was a land of extreme contrast. Grinding poverty existed alongside fantastic wealth. While the Czar and his friends hunted deer in the royal parks, the peasants and workers, burdened by famine, taxation and political oppression, went hungry in silence.

This was the heritage of Vladimir Ilyich Ulyanov, code name Lenin, born in 1870 in a little town on the Volga. While still a boy Lenin came face to face with the full meaning of Czarist autocracy. His rebellious young brother, Alexander, who "had but one aim, to help the unfortunate Russian people," was hanged for revolutionary activities. Lenin, forsaking all loyalty to the Czar, devoted himself to building a new Russia, a Russia free of oppression and injustice. It was to be a lifetime struggle.

This new *History Makers* title tells the story of how Lenin realized his ambitions amidst the intrigues of his opponents and the bitter struggles with the Czar's secret police. It takes the reader through all the exciting ups and downs of Lenin's life in Russia and as an exile in England and other countries. Using much of Lenin's own writings, Lionel Kochan tells the life-story of a man whose battle against autocracy led to the foundation of the world's first communist state.

Lenin

Lionel Kochan

assisted by Miriam Kochan

WAYLAND PUBLISHERS

More Wayland History Makers

The Wright Brothers Russell Ash
Martin Luther King Patricia Baker
Cecil Rhodes Neil Bates
Jomo Kenyatta Julian Friedmann
Rommel F. H. Gregory
Goering F. H. Gregory
Hitler Matthew Holden
Bismarck Richard Kisch
Lenin Lionel Kochan
Al Capone Mary Letts
Karl Marx Caroline Seaward
The Last Czar W. H. C. Smith
Picasso David Sweetman
Captain Scott David Sweetman
The Borgias David Sweetman
Franco Richard Kisch
Joseph Stalin David Hayes and F. H. Gregory
Mao Tse-tung Hugh Purcell
Cromwell Amanda Purves

frontispiece: Lenin in Moscow, July, 1920.

SBN 85340 298 1
Copyright © 1974 by Wayland Publishers Limited
49 Lansdowne Place, Hove, East Sussex BN3 1HF
First published in 1974 by Wayland Publishers Limited
Second impression 1978
Filmset in 'Monophoto' Baskerville and printed in Great Britain by
Page Bros (Norwich) Ltd, Norwich, England

Contents

List of Illustrations

8

1. The Boy

He was a very normal boy. He was naughty and mischievous. He broke his toys and teased his younger brothers and sisters. He had red hair and a head that seemed too big for his sturdy body. There was nothing about him to suggest that one day he would rule over all Russia and that his name would be known all over the world.

His name was not even yet Lenin. He called himself that later. He was christened Vladimir Ilyich Ulyanov when he was born on 20th April, 1870. He grew up in the sleepy Russian town of Simbirsk where his father was an inspector of schools, a job which involved a good deal of travelling. While the father was away, the mother, Maria Alexandrovna, looked after the family of six children.

Vladimir was the third child. All the brothers and sisters seem to have been very fond of one another. In the summer they swam and fished together in the many rivers around Simbirsk (the town itself was actually situated on the largest river in Russia, the Volga). They skated and tobogganed on the rivers when they froze up in the hard Russian winter, and all year round they would take long walks together in the beautiful countryside round about.

But, despite the lovely scenery, all was not well with Russia. The Ulyanovs were not rich but they were

Above **The Ulyanov family's house in Simbirsk.**

Opposite **Lenin as a boy.**

9

"I can trace to my early youth that vague feeling of dissatisfaction with the social system which, penetrating more and more into my consciousness, brought me to the convictions which inspired me in the present case. But only after studying the social and economic sciences did this conviction of the abnormality of the existing system become fully confirmed in me, and the vague dreams of freedom, equality and brotherhood took shape for me in the strictly scientific forms of socialism ..." *Alexander Ulyanov's speech at his trial; March, 1887.*

comfortably off. The father's salary was large enough to keep them in a pleasant roomy wooden house, to feed them adequately and to give them a good education. This was not the case with most of Russia's enormous population. The greater part of them (some 80 million) were peasants who in years when there were bad harvests could barely get enough to eat from their small patches of land. At the other end of the scale, there was a relatively small number of very rich people, owning large estates in the country and beautiful houses in the great Russian cities of Moscow and St. Petersburg.

The richest and most powerful of all was the Czar, the Emperor of Russia, who governed his realm without having to explain his actions to any parliament.

Needless to say, the educated people, who fell somewhere between these two groups, were beginning to criticize this state of affairs. They wanted to have some say in governing the country. The Ulyanovs were certainly educated people. All the family were clever and Vladimir was no exception. This became obvious as soon as he started school at the age of nine and a half. Until then, he had been taught privately at home. At school, he showed himself to be particularly good at languages, but all his marks were excellent. He used to rush home at the end of the day's lessons and tell his delighted father how well he had done.

This happy childhood came to a sudden end for Vladimir when he was fifteen. His father, only fifty-four years old, died suddenly. More trouble came some two years later. His adored elder brother, Sasha (short for Alexander), was one of a group of students arrested by the St. Petersburg police for an unsuccessful attempt to murder the Czar, Alexander III. In a speech at his trial, Sasha said that violence and revolution were the only way to help the unfortunate Russian people. He was hanged in the courtyard of the Schlusselberg fortress on 20th May, 1887.

Above **Peasants begging in the town of Kazan, 1892.**

> **"Lively, pert and jolly and loved loud games, and running around. He broke his toys oftener than he played with them."**
> *Memories of Vladimir, by Anna Ulyanov.*

11

2. The Student

Vladimir studied furiously after this second disaster, promising his mother always to keep well away from any political activity. He would do nothing to bring further tragedy to the small family. He worked so well that he was the star pupil of his year when he left school, winning the gold medal which both his sister, Anna, and poor Sasha had held before him.

Then he went on to the University of Kazan to study law. After the very strict school, university life seemed wonderfully free. But this happy state of affairs did not last long. The Ministry of Education had been frightened by the plot to kill the Czar, and tended to blame the universities, which they saw as breeding grounds for terrorism. The time had come to clamp down on the universities, they decided, and the regulations were made very strict. The students were not prepared to take this lying down. A meeting was called at the University of Kazan to discuss what should be done. Although Vladimir remembered his promise to his mother, he went along to this meeting just to see what would happen. As the students left the hall at the end of the meeting, they found police inspectors at the door taking every student's university registration card.

That night, police knocked on the door of the Ulyanovs' apartment. Disaster had struck again. Along with thirty-nine other students, Vladimir was taken

Above **The University of Kazan.**

Opposite **Lenin as a university student, 1891.**

Above **The jail in Kazan where Lenin was imprisoned in 1887.**

to the police station. He was kept in prison for several days. Then he was expelled from the University of Kazan, ordered to leave the town and to remain under police supervision. Because he was the brother of the rebel, Sasha, the authorities were sure that Vladimir must also be a troublemaker. And they could not afford to have troublemakers going free. "In view of the exceptional circumstances surrounding the Ulyanov family," they reported, "the behaviour of Ulyanov at the meeting gave the inspectors grounds for believing that he was quite capable of various kinds of illegal and criminal demonstrations."

The family disconsolately moved to their country estate at a place called Kukushkino, thirty miles from Kazan. From there, Vladimir and his mother made every effort to obtain permission for him to return to university. He was even prepared to go to a foreign university if he had to, so long as he was allowed to continue his studies. But all their requests were refused.

He did succeed, however, in getting permission to move back to Kazan. He was still determined to qualify as a lawyer and he was delighted to find out that it was possible to do this without going to university. He merely had to take the law exams. Here again, the authorities made difficulties. His mother, equally anxious for her son to take up a solid, sensible profession, wrote innumerable letters to the government pleading as a "widow and a mother" that her son be allowed to take the exams. Finally, consent was given. After a year's tremendously hard work, Vladimir presented himself for examination. He came top of the 124 candidates, most of whom had taken the normal four years to prepare for the examination. By November, 1891, when he was twenty-one years old, he was a full advocate.

"Very gifted, always neat and assiduous, Ulyanov was first in all subjects, and upon completing his studies, received a gold medal as the most deserving pupil with regard to his ability, progress and behaviour. Neither in the school nor outside has a single instance been observed when he has given cause for dissatisfaction, by word or by deed, to the school authorities and teachers..." *Vladimir's school leaving report from Education Chief Fyodor Kerensky, 1887.*

"During his short stay in the university he was conspicuous for his reticence, lack of attention and even rudeness. Only a day or two before the students' meeting he gave grounds for suspicion that he was fermenting trouble..." *Police Report on Vladimir, 1887.*

3. Birth of a Revolutionary

Vladimir had always been a great reader. He read avidly almost every book he could lay his hands on. Now, banished from the university, he had little to do except write letters begging to be allowed to return and open the replies refusing this request. He was even more dependent on literature.

At this low point, when he was eighteen years old, Vladimir made the most important discovery of his life. He picked up a book he remembered Sasha talking about, *Das Kapital.* It was written by a German, Karl Marx. The idea it put forward was that all of history was a movement towards socialism – towards a time when all property would belong to the people and there would be no private ownership. However, this would not just happen of its own accord. It would be the result of a revolution in which the working classes (the industrial workers) would seize power from the capitalist classes (who owned the factories). The government would be overthrown and socialism established.

One can understand why this idea appealed to Vladimir at this point in his career. He himself had suffered (and was still suffering) grievously at the hands of the government. He knew that the conditions in which the Russian workers and peasants lived were anything but satisfactory. He was bowled over by

"I can see him as if it were yesterday sitting on a kitchen stove covered with newspapers and making violent gestures as he spoke of the new horizons which opened out to anyone who followed Marx's theories. There emanated from him a cheerful confidence that was very winning. Even in those early days he had a gift of persuasion, of carrying others with him. Even then he never kept his knowledge to himself, but sought to share it with his friends and win them over to his side." *Memoirs of Vladimir, by Anna Ulyanov.*

Opposite **Members of a poor Russian family.**

17

B

Above **The building in Samara where Lenin lived from 1889 to 1893.**

Karl Marx's book and read it again and again. He could even quote whole paragraphs by heart.

Needless to say, this new interest did not delight his mother. She had visions of Vladimir following in his elder brother's footsteps. She looked around for something to distract him and decided to buy a large farm so that he could become a gentleman farmer. But, transported to the estate she bought him, near the town of Samara on the Volga, Vladimir went on reading. His mother, poor Maria Alexandrovna, had to employ a professional manager to look after the 225 acres. The estate became the family's summer holiday home. For the winter, they rented an apartment in the town of Samara. Here, Vladimir finally lifted his eyes from his books (he was now reading mainly Marxist works on social and economic subjects), and mixed with people who were, like him, followers of Karl Marx. He became a regular member of a study group they held.

Then, as we saw in the previous chapter, he qualified as a lawyer. Not that he was brilliantly successful in this profession. He defended some eight or nine peasants or workers on minor charges. All were found guilty. In any case, he found the job he took in a law office dry and boring. His political activities were of much more interest to him.

His views were now taking on a clearer shape. Russia was hit by famine in 1891. Over most of the country soup kitchens were set up and other forms of relief for the millions of starving peasants were arranged. Vladimir was strongly against this. He felt that every disaster that struck Russia was a blessing. It brought the inevitable revolution one step nearer. Moreover, he explained, the famine was not an act of fate but the result of bad government by the Czar and the capitalist regime.

This was the beginning of Vladimir's split from most

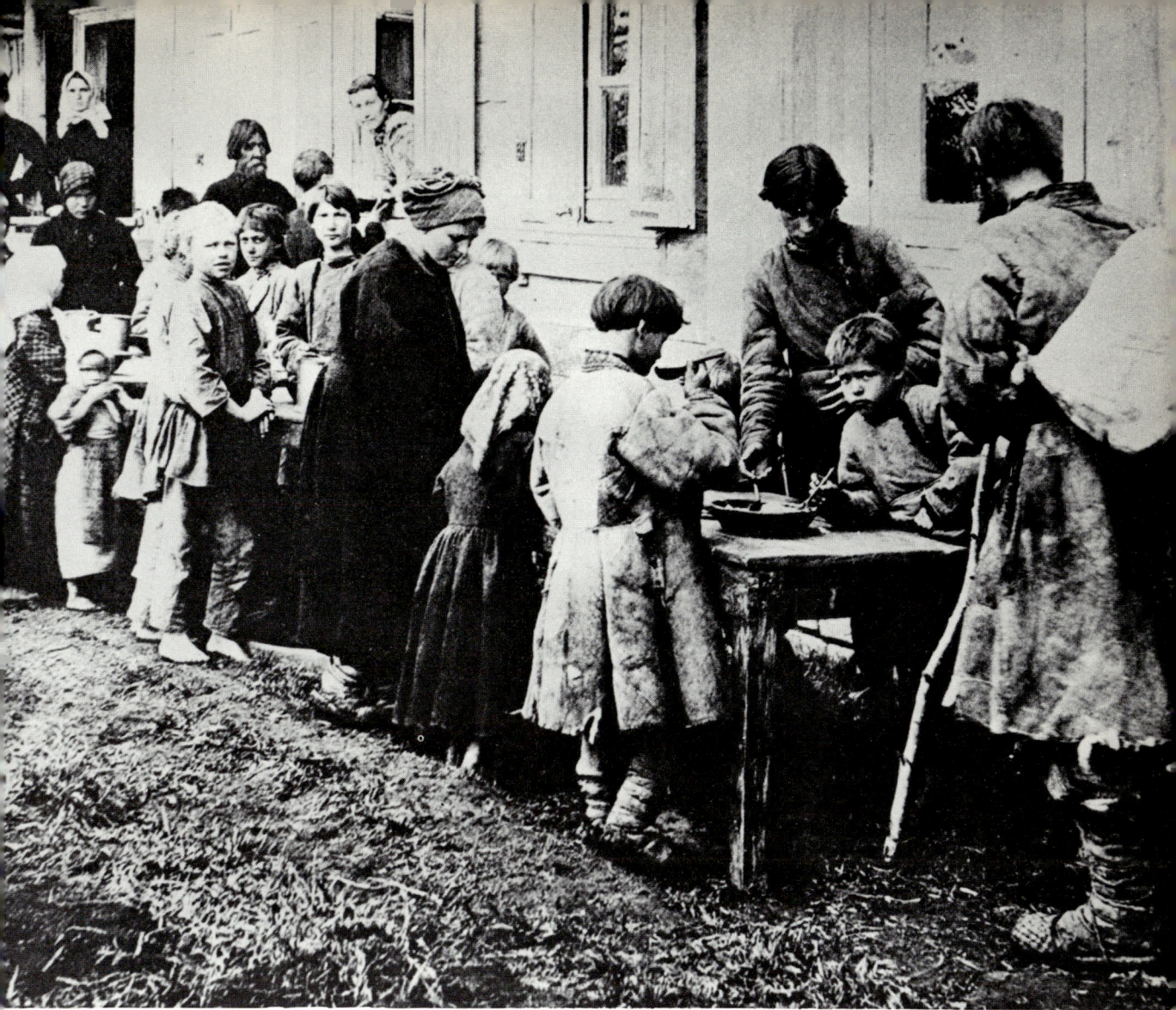

of his fellow revolutionaries. They wanted to help the people there and then. Vladimir felt that the first aim must be to overthrow the government. He became the leader of his own small group of Marxists. He felt that the time had come to leave Samara and try his strength in the Russian capital, St. Petersburg.

Above **A canteen for the poor in Lukoyanovsky district.**

4. St. Petersburg

The Vladimir who arrived in St. Petersburg in 1893 looked like an old man. He was twenty-three years old. He was already almost completely bald, and, as though to make up for this, he had grown a small moustache and a beard. He found a job in a law office where he dutifully worked all day to make enough money to keep himself. In the evenings he began to live.

Vladimir, as we have seen, was convinced that it was the working classes, the industrial workers in the towns, who would make the revolution and overthrow the Czar, even though there were not all that many industrial workers in Russia at that time, compared with the vast numbers of peasants; Russia was still very much an agricultural country. He felt that the first step towards the revolution must be to make these workers thoroughly familiar with revolutionary ideas. He wanted them to understand how powerful they were. If they joined together, they could improve their position and finally free themselves from the slavery of working for capitalists. So, during his free time, Vladimir would walk the streets of St. Petersburg looking for working men. He talked to all those he met about the revolution. He also asked questions of them, writing down what they told him about their wages and living conditions. Whenever he went out on these expeditions, he turned up the collar of his shabby

"His small body, topped by the customary cap, could easily be lost, without attracting attention, in any factory district. A pleasant, dark-complexioned face of a somewhat eastern cast – that is about all that can be said of his outward appearance. Dressed in a cloth coat, Vladimir Ilyich could just as easily remain unnoticed in any crowd of Volga peasants ... But one had only to peer into the eyes of Vladimir Ilyich, into those unusual piercing, dark, dark, brown eyes, full of inner power and energy, to begin to sense that you were face to face with a far from usual type." *Reminiscences of Lenin, by Krzhizhanovsky.*

Opposite **Part of a working class area of St. Petersburg.**

Above **A district in the Urals where workers of an iron and steel works lived.**

overcoat and pulled the workman's cap he wore down over his eyes. In an effort to try to throw any followers off the scent, he used quiet side streets and back alleys. The police were watching his activities carefully, and he knew it. He was not only Sasha's brother now, he was a revolutionary in his own right.

Although his reputation in revolutionary circles was growing, it was not until he made a certain visit to Moscow that he really made his mark. In Moscow, he attended a lecture by a famous revolutionary leader who was attacking Karl Marx's views. Vladimir stood up from his seat at the back of the hall and argued brilliantly in favour of Marx. When he came back to

St. Petersburg after this triumph, everyone had heard about it. After that, he was invited to all Marxist gatherings. At one of them, he met a beautiful, very serious, young girl, named Nadezhda Krupskaya. She worked by his side in all his revolutionary activities.

His main aim at that particular time was to build up an efficient revolutionary organization, able to evade police spies. To do this, he divided the members up into study groups of six, each instructed to agitate amongst the workers. He kept the groups separate from each other. Only he knew about all of them. Whenever any letters had to be written, they had to be in code or invisible ink.

He was also beginning to write pamphlets about Marxist ideas. He was entirely wrapped up in his efforts towards bringing about revolution. And then everything came to a stop. In March, 1895, he caught pneumonia.

Left **Lenin with some fellow revolutionaries, 1897.**

"Accordingly, it is on the working class that the Social Democrats concentrate all their attention and all their energy. When its advanced representatives have appropriated and mastered the ideas of scientific socialism, the idea of the historic mission of the Russian workers, and when these ideas have become widespread, and when enduring organizations have been established among the workers, transforming the present sporadic economic struggle for the workers into conscious class warfare – then the Russian WORKER, having placed himself at the head of all the democratic elements, will overthrow absolutism and lead THE RUSSIAN PROLETARIAT (side by side with the proletariat of ALL COUNTRIES) along the straight road to the VICTORIOUS COMMUNIST REVOLUTION."
What the 'Friends of the People' Are and How They Fight Against the Social Democrats, written in 1894.

5. Abroad

Maria Alexandrovna, Vladimir's mother, was once again the hero of the hour. She had seen her eldest son hanged as a revolutionary, and now Vladimir was in the process of becoming a revolutionary leader. But still she went on indomitably trying to hold the family together.

Most probably, she welcomed Vladimir's illness as a means of halting his revolutionary activity. She hurried to his bedside in St. Petersburg, and, when he had recovered under her care, she packed him off, still thin and pale, to convalesce abroad.

But Vladimir too did not see the trip as being purely for his health. His first stop was Switzerland, where he visited other Russian revolutionary leaders who were living there in exile. They were going to be vitally important to him in the future. In Geneva, he met Georgy Plekhanov, a Marxist who had left Russia twelve years earlier. The two men found that their ideas were very different. Both believed in the revolution but Vladimir thought that it could only be brought about by violence. Plekhanov believed that persuading people by reasoning with them was a better way. "You show the bourgeois your behind," Vladimir told the older man, "we, on the contrary, look them in the face."

Vladimir got on better with a man called Paul

"As Lenin worked abroad shoulder to shoulder with Plekhanov, and as what the Germans call 'the pathos of distance' vanished, it must have become physically clear to the 'pupil' that he not only had nothing more to learn from the teacher about the question which he then considered fundamental, but that the sceptical, critical teacher, thanks to his authority, was in a position to hinder his rescue work and to separate him from the younger colleagues."
Lenin, by Leon Trotsky.

Opposite **Lenin in Moscow, 1900.**

25

Axelrod. They made many important decisions together as they walked and talked in the hills around Zurich. Firstly, they agreed that all the groups who wanted to overthrow the Czar and his government should get together and form a common front. Then, they decided that all Vladimir's small study groups should be turned into one big Russian political party. Lastly, they resolved to start a political magazine to be printed abroad and sent to the workers in Russia.

Vladimir then began to enjoy his first trip abroad. He stayed in Paris for a month, wandering round and marvelling at the beauty of the city. Then, after a brief return to Switzerland, he went on to Germany. He took an apartment in Berlin, bathed regularly in the River Spree for his health and read in the Royal Library.

By September, Vladimir decided that his "holiday" had lasted long enough. Although letters from his mother warned him not to hurry home, he was back in St. Petersburg that month.

He began to understand his mother's warnings as soon as he reached the Russian frontier. His luggage was very carefully examined by the guards there. To his great relief, they did not find out that his trunk had a false bottom. In it, he had hidden a printing machine and a pile of illegal pamphlets.

But his relief did not last long. Because police spies kept a very close watch on him in St. Petersburg, he had to send his letters to Plekhanov and Axelrod in Switzerland hidden in the bindings of books which he then sent by parcel post. His letters were full of news at that time because a wave of strikes was taking place amongst the St. Petersburg workers – perhaps revolution was in the air? Messages from Switzerland reached Vladimir in the same way.

Things came to a head on 20th December, 1895. Vladimir and some of his fellow Marxists were in

Krupskaya's apartment. The first issue of a newspaper they planned to distribute amongst the workers was ready to go to the printers. Suddenly, they heard a sharp knock at the door. Before they could answer it, a crowd of policemen entered the room. Vladimir and his crowd of revolutionary friends were taken to the police station.

Above **Striking workers of the Lysva metallurgical plant, Perm province.**

6. Prison

Vladimir was thrown into a small cell in the House of Preliminary Detention. He stayed there for a year. On the surface he behaved like a model prisoner – he gave no trouble and he obeyed all the rules. In reality, however, he was making full use of his past experience of secret communication. Not only did he manage to write letters to his friends and receive replies, he also wrote articles which were circulated in St. Petersburg.

How was this possible? His methods varied. Sometimes the books he borrowed had dots over certain letters when he returned them. Sometimes, he wrote and received messages written in milk. Such messages are invisible until the paper is held over a candle flame. Although Vladimir had no candle in his cell, he found he could obtain the desired result by plunging the message into his prison mug of hot tea.

Things improved for him in February, 1897. He was released from prison and exiled for three years to Siberia, in the far north of Russia. Strange as it may seem, life for political exiles in Siberia was not too unpleasant at this time. Although they were forced to stay away from large cities, they were allowed to live a more or less normal life.

And Vladimir did. Hunting and fishing with his fellow exiles, he enjoyed the country life in the pretty village of Shushenskoye to which he was sent. But he

"The farther east we go in Europe, the weaker, more abject and cowardly does the bourgeoisie become politically, and the greater the cultural and political tasks which devolve upon the proletariat. On its strong shoulders the Russian working class must and will carry the work of conquering political liberty. This is an essential step, but only the first step, to a realization of the great historic mission of the proletariat, to the foundation of a social order in which there will be no place for the exploitation of man by man." *Manifesto of the Russian Social Democratic Workers' Party, 1898.*

Opposite **Lenin's cell in the St. Petersburg Remand Prison.**

Above **Lenin hunting, a drawing by V. N. Nikolsky.**

"My health is satisfactory. I can have mineral water here; it is brought to me from a pharmacy the day I order it. I sleep about nine hours a day and dream about the various chapters of my future books." *Lenin, in a letter to Anna from prison, 1896.*

did not neglect his work. His exile gave him a chance to finish a book on capitalism which he was writing, and he continued to send his articles and pamphlets to St. Petersburg for publication. He also opened his own law office to give free legal advice to poor people. Of the news from the big city that reached him, one item that particularly pleased him was that a Russian Social Democratic Workers' Party had been formed. In March, 1898, ten representatives had met in the town of Minsk for this purpose. They called their meeting the first Congress of the Russian Communist Party. The aim of the party was to overthrow the Czar and bring about socialism through the workers.

Less happy news was that Krupskaya had been

arrested in St. Petersburg. Fortunately, however, Vladimir was able to get permission for her to join him in Siberia instead of going to prison. The sole condition was his promise that they would get married. So Vladimir and Krupskaya set up house together in Shushenskoye. Krupskaya's mother also came along, and ran the house for the young couple while they got on with their work for the revolution.

Vladimir never let his love for his new bride interfere with his political interests. As the years of exile dragged on, he could not wait to get back into active political life. When his exile at last ended in January, 1900, he left Krupskaya (she still had a year left to serve), and headed straight back to St. Petersburg.

> **"I'm in a far better position than most of the citizens of Russia. They can never find me."**
> *Lenin, in a letter to his mother from prison.*

7. "The Spark"

In theory, Vladimir was not allowed to stay in St. Petersburg itself, or even to go into the city. So he chose to settle in a small town called Pskov, a hundred miles from the capital and near the Russian border. This was useful for smuggling in forbidden pamphlets and papers.

He joyfully went back to a life of underground activity, disguises and dodging the police. He paid several visits to St. Petersburg, each time wearing a different disguise and going by a different and very roundabout route. Sometimes, he took along his friend Julius Martov, whom he had met during his exile. On one of these trips, Vladimir was arrested by the police, even though he had changed trains at practically every station to throw his followers off the trail. He was kept in prison for a fortnight and then allowed to go free. But this incident was enough to show him that he could carry on his work much more easily outside Russia.

What exactly was this work? The task Vladimir had set himself was once again to publish a secret revolutionary newspaper. He wanted this to be something that the workers would find interesting and which would encourage them to go on strike against their employers and the government. Before Vladimir left Russia, the name of this paper had been decided. It was to be called *Iskra* (which means *The Spark*). Its editors, Vladimir,

"I used to work in a circle that set itself very wide, all-embracing tasks, and all of us who were members of the circle suffered to the point of actual torture from the consciousness that we were proving ourselves to be such amateurs . . . since then, whenever I have remembered the burning sense of shame I experienced, my bitterness towards the pseudo-Social Democrats was increased, because their teachings disgrace the calling of 'a revolutionary' and because they fail to understand that our task is not to effect the degradation of the revolutionary to the level of the amateur, but to *raise* the amateur to the level of the revolutionary." *What is to be Done?*, *by Lenin.*

Opposite **Pskov. The room in which Lenin lived in 1900.**

c

Above **Russian refugees printing "illegal" material in Paris, 1906.**

Martov, and another former exile, Potresov, hoped it would kindle the revolutionary spark amongst the Russian workers.

Vladimir left for Switzerland to discuss final plans for the paper with the Swiss–Russian revolutionaries. Here he at once ran into trouble. At their first meeting, he and Plekhanov had found it hard to agree. Now, they discovered that their ideas about *Iskra* were very different. Plekhanov wanted the paper to be one which would simply encourage people to argue about ideas. Vladimir hoped to make it into a practical tool for reorganizing the Social Democratic Party. Finally, however, they reached some sort of agreement. A six-man editorial board was set up. To get away from Plekhanov, Vladimir arranged for the paper to be printed in Germany, and he later moved to Munich to be near the printer. Krupskaya joined him there when her sentence had ended.

The first issues of *Iskra* printed there were quite clearly Vladimir's work. It was in them that the name "Lenin" first appeared underneath the articles he wrote. From that time on, he was to be referred to more and more often by that name.

At the same time, he was writing a book called *What is to be Done?* It explained that the working classes could not bring about the revolution by themselves. They might be satisfied with small improvements in their living conditions, like higher wages or shorter working hours, (the Economist Party in Russia was at that time trying to obtain this sort of change), but, by themselves, they might not bother to aim at revolution. For the revolution to be successful, it had to be led by a group of full-time revolutionaries. They would be specially trained men who would devote themselves solely to the revolution.

What is to be Done? was published in March, 1902. In the same month, the German printers decided that it was too dangerous for them to go on printing *Iskra*. For Lenin and his wife, another move was necessary.

Above **The first issue of** *Iskra* (*The Spark*).

"Don't you know that at Czarskoe-Selo there's an agent behind every bush?" *A police inspector to Lenin.*

8. On the Move

Lenin and Krupskaya brought *Iskra* to a London shrouded in dense fog. But they settled down happily, and Lenin set about learning English. He also took out a reader's ticket to the British Museum library in the name of Jacob Richter, and spent most of his mornings quietly reading there.

They found quite a large colony of Russian revolutionaries in London. Lenin's small two-roomed flat at 30, Holford Square, Kings Cross, became a centre where they all gathered to drink lemon tea and talk. His landlady, Mrs. Yeo, charged him the equivalent of $12\frac{1}{2}$p a week. One of their visitors was a twenty-two-year-old fugitive from Irkutsk in Russia, called Leon Davydovitch Bronstein. His passport was made out in the name of Leon Trotsky. Later, he played an important part in events in Russia.

This happy period did not last long. After less than a year, the editorial committee of *Iskra* decided that it was absurd to have half its members in London and the other half in Switzerland. So, in April, 1903, Lenin and Krupskaya packed their bags once again.

It was a thin, delicate-looking man who moved into the small house in Secheron, a working-class suburb of Geneva. Lenin had found all the moving around a great strain. People who saw him at that time said he had an enormous bald head, a long, silky, red beard,

"Lenin behaved – according to his own expression – like a madman. True. He banged the door. True. His conduct aroused the indignation of the members who remained at the meeting. So it did! But what follows? Only that my arguments on the substance of the questions in dispute were convincing and were borne out during the course of the congress." *One Step Forward, Two Steps Back, 1904 – Lenin's answer to Martov's criticisms.*

Opposite **The house where Lenin lived in London.**

Above **Lenin addressing the Second Congress of the Social Democratic Party.**

and the drooping moustaches then in fashion.

Soon he was going to need all his strength. The Second Congress of the Social Democratic Party was held in a warehouse in Brussels that summer, and socialists from many European countries attended it. Here, Lenin really made his mark as a leader. He presented his plan for the revolution, insisting that the members of the Congress agreed to every detail of it. There was one violent quarrel after another. In the middle of it all, the Belgian police forbade the continuance of the Congress on Belgian soil. The meeting broke up and quickly reassembled in London, to continue arguing.

The members could not agree on anything. Some walked out. They did not like Lenin's idea that the revolutionary party must be controlled by a central committee. All the groups that belonged to it would have had to obey the decisions of the top leaders. Those that walked out were not prepared to do this. Even his friends, Trotsky and Martov, were against Lenin now. They thought he was wrong to want a professional revolutionary party that would seize power for the working classes. In their opinion, the party should be open to anyone who believed in its programme. They also felt that any party members should have the right to vote in party affairs.

But Lenin was determined to get his own way. He was rude and domineering. He bullied and insulted people. He would not give way an inch. And he won. Those who voted on his side (and to his surprise, his old enemy Plekhanov was one of them), he called Bolsheviks (which means "majority"). Those who voted against him, he called Mensheviks (minority).

"He who enters danger, that man will be the professional revolutionary." *Lenin's notes made during the 2nd Congress of the Social Democratic Party, 1903.*

9. "Forward"

Lenin had won, but he did not get much satisfaction from his victory. His aggressive behaviour at the Congress had made him much disliked. He seemed to have enemies all around him. They even had the upper hand on the editorial board of his newspaper, *Iskra*. Feeling that he could not work in this sort of situation, Lenin resigned from his job on the newspaper.

He did not, however, resign from revolutionary politics. He decided to publish a new newspaper called *Vperyod (Forward)*. It would be a real revolutionary publication. It would not be a tool of the "so-called ambassadors of the working class, Plekhanov, Martov and the rest," which is how he now regarded *Iskra*.

He brought out the first issue of *Vperyod* in January, 1905, before he really had enough money to pay for it. There was method in this apparent madness. The news he was receiving from Russia showed that the Russian people there were very discontented with the Czar's government. A war between Russia and Japan had broken out in 1904. Most Russians had not wanted the war in the first place, and they wanted it even less when they heard that their country was losing battle after battle. Lenin hoped that *Vperyod* would increase this discontent until it finally grew into revolution.

In part, his hopes were justified. Three weeks after the first issue of *Vperyod* appeared, police and soldiers

"The military collapse is now inevitable, and together with it there will come inevitably a tenfold increase of unrest, discontent and rebellion. For that moment we must prepare with all energy. At that moment one of those outbreaks, which are recurring, now here, now there, with such growing frequency, will develop into a tremendous popular movement. At that moment the proletariat will rise to take its place at the head of the insurrection to win freedom for the entire people and to secure for the working classes the possibility of waging an open and broad struggle for socialism, a struggle enriched by the whole experience of Europe."
An extract from the first issue of Vperyod.

Opposite **Wounded Russian soldiers returning to St. Petersburg from the Russo-Japanese War, September, 1904.**

Right **"Bloody Sunday." The procession to the Winter Palace dispersed by gunfire.**

"The prestige of the Czarist name has been ruined forever. The uprising has begun, force against force. Street fighting has begun, barricades have been thrown up, rifle fire is crackling, guns are cannonading. Blood flows in rivers, and a civil war for freedom is blazing. Moscow and the South, the Caucasus and Poland are ready to join forces with the Petersburg proletariat. The slogan of the workers is: Death or Freedom!"

Extract from Vperyod's editorial after the events of Bloody Sunday, January, 1905.

fired on a crowd of 200,000 people in front of the Winter Palace in St. Petersburg. The people had marched there quite peacefully to petition the Czar, now Nicholas II, for better conditions for the workers, but those who were left alive felt anything but peaceful. When Lenin heard about the events of Bloody Sunday, as the fateful day was called, he was delighted. He went to a Geneva cafe kept by Russian exiles and sang a revolutionary funeral march in honour of the dead.

You can imagine how difficult Lenin found it to stay quietly in Geneva at this time. The Russian papers told him that in the countryside the peasants were attacking landlords' houses, and that more and more workers were striking. And he could do nothing. It was even worse for him to learn that a number of his fellow exiles, like Trotsky, had managed to get back to Russia and were becoming leaders of the revolt.

Why did Lenin too not try to get back to Russia to lead the revolution? No-one really knows. He probably felt that his most important task was to lead and plan the revolution from a distance. He also could not believe that this was really the socialist revolution. If anything, it was only a preparation for it. So, chafing with impatience in Geneva, all he could do was continue to write *Vperyod* and send it on to the workers in Russia. He also called a Congress of the Social Democratic Party in London in April. He only invited the Bolsheviks (the people who agreed with his views) to this. The Mensheviks held their own conference at the same time in the Swiss capital.

He made a few pathetic attempts to help the Russian revolt from a distance. For example, he arranged for a load of arms to be sent to the workers in Russia, but the boat carrying them ran aground and blew up. Again, in June, 1905, there was a mutiny on a Russian ship, the *Prince Potemkin,* in Odessa. Lenin sent one of his followers to Odessa to turn the mutiny into a rebellion. By the time the man got there, the mutiny was over.

In autumn, 1905, Lenin could stand it no longer. He left Krupskaya and set off for Russia.

Below **Officers and men of the battleship** *Prince Potemkin.*

10. Phony Revolution

Various things happened in Russia before Lenin finally got back there. The country was hit by a general strike. Nearly all the workers had left their jobs – bus drivers, factory hands, railway men, everybody. The life of St. Petersburg was at a standstill. The workers had set up "Soviets," councils of all the workers in the city. At first, these were only meant to organize the strike, but they soon got stronger and more powerful. The Czar was so worried by all these developments that he agreed to everything the workers asked for. On 17th October he issued the October Manifesto. This announced that Russia was to have its first elected parliament, the Duma, and promised freedom of speech and other political rights. Most important for Lenin, it pardoned all Russian political exiles.

Lenin could now come back to Russia without fear of being arrested by the police. In November, 1905, he was home. He felt completely out of touch with all the events that were taking place. He saw that a revolution was indeed in process, but it was not happening in the way he had expected. Many things about it did not please him. For example, Trotsky was at the head of the St. Petersburg Soviet, and Trotsky was a Menshevik. Also, the Soviets which had taken power represented the workers – they were far from being the professional revolutionaries Lenin thought should lead the

"The Cadets are the worms in the grave of the revolution. The revolution lies buried. The worms gnaw at it. But the revolution has the power of coming quickly to life again and of blossoming forth magnificently on the well-turned soil. Splendidly and marvellously has the soil been turned during the October days of freedom and the December uprising. And we are far from denying that the worms perform a useful work in this age when the revolution lies buried. Look how well these greasy worms are preparing the soil . . ."
The Victory of the Cadets, 1906.

Opposite **A crowd demonstrating in Moscow for the release of political prisoners, 1905.**

revolution.

Because of this, he did not take much part in active politics at this time, even when, in the spring of 1906, the first elections of members of the Duma was held. However, he was obviously upset when a political group called the Cadets (short for the Constitutional Democrats) gained the largest number of votes. They were much less extreme than the Bolsheviks and even the Mensheviks. Lenin wrote an angry pamphlet about the victory of the Cadets, but he may as well have saved his breath. The Cadets never succeeded in forming a government.

All the time he was in Russia on this occasion, he felt he was being closely watched by secret police. He changed his passport every few weeks to dodge them. His days in St. Petersburg were steeped in conspiracy, collecting secret stores of fire-arms and holding secret meetings. This secrecy was probably unnecessary. Since the October Manifesto, everyone was much freer than before to come and go as they pleased in Russia. But conspiracy had become a habit with Lenin. It was another sign of how out of touch he was with what was going on.

Never happy unless he was running a newspaper to tell the workers his ideas on the revolution, he took over yet another, called *Novaya Zhizn* (*New Life*). A poet called Vilenkin, who worked on the paper, said that Lenin (who was thirty-five at that time) looked like a minor civil servant. "He was always ungainly, ill-dressed, rather stoop-shouldered, and you would never believe that this bald man with the impenetrable Mongoloid features and slow deliberate movements was one of the most completely fearless, skilful and determined men of our time. It was only when you looked carefully at his sharp narrow eyes and un-forgettable smile that you perceived the extraordinary willpower concealed behind the very ordinary mask of his face."

> "No, comrades, you must not believe that the workers should support the Cadets; that would be like saying that the function of steam is not to drive the ship's engine but to blow the ship's siren." *The Victory of the Cadets, 1906.*

Left **The Workers Council of St. Petersburg, whose members were sent to Siberia in December, 1905. (Trotsky is marked with a cross).**

11. Retreat

The general strike faded out. Slowly, the hungry workers went back to work. The Czar was able to return to his old policy. He arrested the men who had led the strikes in the towns, even the heads of the St. Petersburg Soviet. He punished the peasants in the country who had raided their landlords' estates, and sent troops in to break up an uprising in Moscow by force. The phony revolution had died.

But in Lenin's mind it was not dead. He continued to scheme and plot – sometimes in Russia but mostly in Finland, for he was once again a "wanted" man, and had to avoid the secret police in earnest.

In Finland, he stayed in a large rambling house near a railway station in a place called Kukkala. There he avidly read every bit of news from Russia that he could lay his hands on. He also continued to write his articles for the revolutionary press. One of these landed him in more trouble than he had bargained for. This article was called "The St. Petersburg Elections and the Hypocrisy of the 31 Mensheviks." It accused the Mensheviks of crawling on their bellies to make peace with the Cadets. The Mensheviks, incensed by Lenin's criticisms, ordered him to stand trial for "conduct impermissible in a party member" before a court of the Social Democratic Party (because Bolsheviks and Mensheviks were still members of the same Social

"Vladimir Ilyich Lenin stood before me even more firm and more inflexible than he had been at the London Congress. In those days he had been very agitated, and there were moments when it was obvious that the party split had given him a difficult time. Now he was in a quiet, rather cold and mocking mood, sternly rejecting all philosophical conversations and altogether on the alert.

"And at the same time there was in Capri another Lenin – a wonderful companion and lighthearted person with a lively and inexhaustible interest in the world around him, and very gentle in his relations with people." *Maxim Gorki on Lenin's visit to Capri.*

Opposite Policemen searching a "suspect" passer-by in a street in 1905.

D

Democratic Party). Nine party members acted as judges to try Lenin's case. He told them that his actions were quite justified, as all means were permissible in a disunited party (and the Social Democratic Party was certainly disunited!). He explained that any methods could be used to fight an enemy – whether that enemy was the Czar or people who did not agree with Lenin. He was actually putting these words into action. The Bolsheviks were getting money to pay for their activities by robbing banks and by other doubtful means.

It may seem surprising after this episode, but Bolsheviks and Mensheviks were once again sitting at the same conference table in London at the end of

Below **Maxim Gorki's villa on Capri, where he received Lenin in 1910.**

April, 1907. After this conference, Lenin went back to Finland absolutely exhausted. But he was not able to rest and recover for long, as the police were after him again. He felt that it would be better to leave Finland, but this was easier said than done. In the end, he walked three miles at night over thin ice to an island where a steamer picked him up. He was not to see Russia again for nine years.

At first he settled in Switzerland, where he and Krupskaya lived in a dreary room in Geneva. His articles continued to appear, now in his new paper called *Proletary*. But he was terribly bored. Krupskaya complained that they simply did not know what to do with themselves in the evenings. However, they did take the odd holiday. On one occasion, they went to Capri to visit a great Russian revolutionary writer, Maxim Gorki. Gorki had started a university there for Russian revolutionary exiles. Lenin was very interested in this though Gorki himself was not a Bolshevik.

Lenin was so impressed that he followed Gorki's example. In the spring of 1911, he set up his own school for training underground workers. It was in Longjumeau on the outskirts of Paris, to which he and Krupskaya had now moved. He rented two small rooms from a leather-worker. There he gave lectures on political economy, the agrarian question and the practice of socialism.

Above **Lenin in Paris, 1910.**

12. The Bolshevik Party

Lenin had never been more alone in his political position than at this time. The 1905 revolution had failed. The workers in Russia were tired out and depressed as a result, uninterested in revolutionary propaganda. The Social Democratic Party was as usual divided by the violent quarrels between Bolsheviks and Mensheviks. Worst of all, Lenin now had to cope with a split in his own small Bolshevik Party. Members were quarrelling about complex questions of philosophy.

So Lenin decided to make a complete break. He would no longer work for a Social Democratic Party which included all the quarrelling Bolsheviks and Mensheviks as well as other revolutionary groups. Instead, he would concentrate all his efforts on building up a separate Bolshevik Party of his own.

As a first step towards doing this, he called a Social Democratic Party conference in Prague in January, 1912. Almost all the people who attended it were his own followers. They elected a new Central Committee which was to have supreme power in the Social Democratic Party. It alone, they said, had the right to represent the Russian working classes. All communications to the Social Democratic Party must be addressed to the Central Committee through its Chairman, Vladimir Ulyanov – Lenin.

Of course, the Mensheviks were absolutely furious

"The arrangement is such that the delegates at the conference will vote with complete uniformity, and therefore in the interests of party unity it would be better if I had no part in it."
Plekhanov's reply to Lenin's invitation to the Prague Conference in 1912.

Opposite **Lenin walking in the outskirts of a Polish town, 1914.**

about this. What Lenin had done was to more or less take over the Social Democratic Party. This was another time when he followed his policy of the end justifying the means. He did not mind how badly he behaved or how many people he offended, the main thing for him was the revolution. And the revolution had to proceed exactly the way he planned it.

The Prague Conference announced the aims it was fighting for; it wanted an eight-hour working day in Russia, which was to be made a democratic republic, and the large estates were to be taken away from the rich landlords and divided up amongst the poor peasants.

But the fulfilment of all these aims would take time. In the meantime, the conference called for armed revolt in Russia. It advised its members to make contact with the Russian fleet in the Baltic and try and get the sailors interested in the revolution. They should also do their best to smuggle arms, guns and ammunition into Russia.

The aims the conference announced caught the fancy of the Russian workers. They particularly liked the idea of an eight-hour working day. As a result, more and more Russians joined the Bolshevik Party, which was becoming quite well established. It had six members of its own in the Duma, its own separate organization and its own newspaper.

As for Lenin, as soon as the conference was over, he set about carrying out its advice. This was not easy living in Switzerland, as he did. He decided to move nearer to Russia. He and Krupskaya therefore moved to Cracow in Austria, near the Russian frontier.

"You ask me why I am in Austria. The Central Committee has set up a bureau here (*entre nous*); we are close to the frontier and will take advantage of it. Also we are nearer to St. Petersburg, and it is much easier to write articles for the papers in Russia, and collaboration is being arranged. There is less wrangling, and that too is an advantage. There is no good library, and that is a disadvantage. It is hard to live without books." *Lenin to Gorki, summer, 1914.*

Opposite **A general view of the town of Cracow.**

13. War and Revolution

Lenin must have been one of the few Russians who was happy when what was to become known as the Great War broke out in August, 1914. It was between Germany and Austria on one side, and Russia, France, Italy and England on the other. Lenin saw it as a fight between the capitalist powers. They would destroy each other, and the way would then be clear for the revolution. This revolution would be international. The war between the nations would change into a war between the classes.

Lenin was living in Cracow when the war was declared. As a Russian living on Austrian soil, he was immediately arrested and his house was searched. After spending twelve days in prison, he was set free on condition that he left the country.

He and Krupskaya returned to Switzerland. They settled first in Berne and later in Zurich. Lenin's excitement about the war subsided as the months dragged on. He was very disappointed when he found that many of his fellow-revolutionaries were joining the army and fighting for their own countries. This was a far cry from Lenin's idea of the workers of the world fighting together against the capitalists, regardless of nationality. "The workers have no fatherland," Karl Marx had said in the *Communist Manifesto*, but, in a war situation, Lenin's fellow-revolutionaries paid no

"Suddenly, before the eyes of all of us, completely overwhelmed by the vulgar routines of revolutionary work, there was presented a bright, dazzling and exotic light which obliterated everything we lived by. Lenin's voice, coming straight from the train, was 'a voice from the outside.' Upon us – in the midst of the revolution – there broke a music which was not at all dissonant, but was new and brusque and rather deafening." *Sukhanov, a journalist of the time, reports Lenin's speech on his return to Russia in April, 1917.*

Opposite **Dead Russian soldiers guarded by Germans, May, 1919.**

57

Above **Czar Nicholas II.**

heed to this. By the end of 1916 he was becoming truly disheartened. He said: "We, the old ones [he was forty-six at the time], may never live to see the decisive battles of the coming revolution."

Only a few months later, in February, 1917, revolution broke out in Russia. Again it was not the work of a picked band of trained revolutionaries. It was brought about by the working classes themselves. They were finding it terribly hard to get food because of the war, and they were horrified by the enormous number of casualties the war was claiming. Disgust at the way the Czar was mis-managing the war was widespread.

On 23rd February, 1917, 90,000 workers came out on strike in St. Petersburg (which had been re-named Petrograd). The next day, the number rose to 200,000. Nicholas II ordered his soldiers to force the people back to work, but, to his horror, the soldiers, who were equally tired of the war, joined the workers instead. There was nothing the Czar could do. He gave up his throne and abdicated.

But the country still had to be governed. A Provisional Government was set up in the Duma. At the same time, the Petrograd Workers' Soviet was formed again, and these two bodies began to rule Russia together.

It took a long time for news to get from Russia to Switzerland, particularly in war-time. Lenin, still in Zurich, did not hear about these events until several days later. The news threw him into a fury of impatience. Again he had not been present at the decisive moment. Again the Bolshevik party in Russia had played very little part in the revolution. Lenin was determined that he himself and his party would be well to the fore in the next stage. In his opinion, this revolution was only a first stage. The next stage would be the overthrow of the Provisional Government by the working classes, and Lenin would be their leader. But to lead the revolution Lenin had to get back to Russia. How was he going to leave Switzerland? Europe was still in the midst of the Great War. France and Italy – two of the countries bordering on Switzerland – were not going to let Lenin cross their lands. They knew of his ambition to bring about an international revolution. Germany – Switzerland's third neighbour – was at war with Russia. Would Germany let this Russian citizen inside its boundaries?

Germany would. She wanted Russia to leave the war and so leave her with only the western powers to tackle. From Germany's point of view, there was much to be gained from letting Lenin go back to Russia. A successful revolution in Russia would make it more or less impossible for that country to fight a war properly. In any case, if Lenin came to power he would not want his country to take part in a "capitalist" war.

There was one problem however. Lenin did not want the Russian people to know that he had accepted help from their enemy, Germany, so, after a great deal of thought, it was decided that Lenin should return to Russia across Germany in a "sealed" train. He should have no contact with Germans or Germany throughout the long journey.

On the afternoon of 9th April, 1917, Lenin, Krupskaya and twenty leading Bolsheviks boarded the train that was to take them home. For four days and nights they saw and spoke to no-one else. On the fourth day, they reached the German frontier town of Sassnitz. They left the train which had almost become a home for them, and crossed by a ferry-boat to Sweden. Just one more train journey – and they would be home.

As he drew nearer to Russia, Lenin became more and more restless. What would he find when he arrived?

"The war is being waged for the division of colonies and the robbery of foreign territories; thieves have fallen out – and to refer to the defeats at a given moment of one of the thieves in order to identify the interests of the thieves with the interests of the nation or the fatherland, is an unconscionable bourgeois lie." *Lenin, 1914.*

Overleaf **Lenin's arrival in Petrograd, 3rd April, 1917. A painting by K. Aksenov.**

Would he be arrested the moment he set foot in the land? At 11 p.m. on 16th April, his questions were answered. As he stepped off the train, a tremendous shout arose from the platform. Thousands of people had gathered at the Finland station (Petrograd's central station) to welcome him. The platform was a blaze of light and colour. Search-lights beamed down on a sea of red banners waving in the air. The whole station was decorated with red and gold ribbons. A band struck up the French revolutionary anthem, the *Marseillaise*. A young naval officer walked forward to welcome Lenin on behalf of the citizens of Petrograd.

Below **Lenin stating his April Theses, 1917.**

It was truly a hero's welcome.

He spent the next twenty-four hours at political conferences and giving speeches, announcing the main points of his policy to his fellow revolutionaries. The policy statement which became known as Lenin's April Theses shocked everyone. He said in the first place that the system of "double power" (whereby the country was ruled by both the Provisional Government and the Soviets) must go. All power must rest with the Soviets. Secondly, there was a need for strong anti-war propaganda. Thirdly, that the large estates should immediately be taken away from the landlords and handed over to the Committees for the poor peasantry. Finally, he wanted the name of his party to be changed. It should now be called the "Communist" Party. No-one should be allowed to belong to it who did not accept completely all of Lenin's ideas.

Lenin had to fight very hard before his fellow-revolutionaries agreed to these points. Once they had agreed, all that remained to do was to wait for the right moment to overthrow the Provisional Government. Lenin was good at waiting.

> **"For us Russians from the point of view of the working classes of Russia, there is not the slightest doubt, absolutely no doubt that the least evil would be now and immediately – the defeat of Czarism in this war. For Czarism is a hundred times worse than Kaiserism."** *Lenin, October, 1914.*

> **"No objections to the transit of Russian revolutionaries if effected in special train with reliable escort. Organization can be worked out between representatives of IIIb (Military Passport Office) and Foreign Ministry.** *Telegram to Foreign Ministry in Berlin from German High Command, 23rd March, 1917.*

14. Waiting

Lenin had no time to become impatient while he waited for the overthrow of the Provisional Government. The following weeks were full of events.

The workers, peasants and soldiers were becoming more and more dissatisfied with the Provisional Government. As far as they were concerned, the revolution had not made life much better for them. Food was still terribly short and prices were high. The peasants in the countryside were restless. In June and July, 1917, many of them took possession of estate owners' land by force. Another cause for discontent was that Russia was still taking part in the Great War. In the summer, the Provisional Government made a tremendous effort to launch a heavy attack on the Germans. It hoped that a major victory would cheer the people at home and take their minds off their other problems. The attack was duly made. It ended in a crashing defeat for the Russians. The ordinary soldiers, weary of the war, were further disturbed by the appointment of an extreme right-wing officer, General Kornilov, as their commander-in-chief.

There were demonstrations right through this period. They began as early as May, when rioting took place in the streets of Petrograd. Another disturbance occurred in June when a march was planned on the Maryinsky Palace where the Provisional Government

Above **A Moscow crowd gathering to hear a Bolshevik speaker.**

Opposite **Lenin disguised with a wig and cap.**

E

> **"All revolutions which have taken place up to the present have helped to perfect the state machinery, whereas it must be shattered, broken to pieces. This conclusion is the chief and fundamental thesis of the Marxist theory of the State."**
> *The State and Revolution, by Lenin.*

Below **This forged passport with a picture of Lenin in disguise enabled him to escape to Finland in 1917.**

Forged passport with picture of himself in disguise enabled Lenin to escape to Finland in the fall of 1917. Warrant for his arrest had been issued in July of that same year.

was meeting. In the following month, there was yet another uprising. However, the Provisional Government was able to restore peace on all three occasions.

No-one knows whether or not Lenin helped to organize all these disturbances. We do know that many Bolsheviks supported them, and were also blamed for them. After the July riots, the Provisional Government raided the Bolshevik Party headquarters, arrested many leading Bolsheviks and issued an order for the arrest of Lenin.

Once more, Lenin donned a workman's cap, borrowed an old raincoat, and went into hiding, this time in a working class district of Petrograd. He called himself Konstantin Ivanov. And this was the man who had been a hero just a few weeks before! Now he was not very popular. The Provisional Government wanted to arrest him for causing the uprisings. The people were disappointed because the riots had failed, and that their leader had deserted them. Why, they asked, did he not give himself up to the Provisional Government? He would then have to stand trial in a court of law. What a wonderful chance to state the Bolshevik case!

But Lenin preferred to lie low. He may have been afraid that his dealings with the German government might come to light if his past was investigated. It was unfortunate that at this time some documents had been published which suggested that he might be a German agent. This did not add to his popularity.

Lenin moved from one hiding place to another. He slept in haylofts and barns. He shaved off his beard and grew tanned and healthy from the open-air country life he was leading. Eventually he arrived in Finland. Here he settled down in the house of a Bolshevik police-chief in Helsingfors. He wrote a book there, *The State and Revolution*, in which he tried to work out what would happen after the revolution, and planned out his own revolution as precisely as a military operation. He continued to write articles, which were taken back to Petrograd by messenger, and read every Russian newspaper he could find.

There was plenty to read about. Events were moving fast in Petrograd. In September, the Provisional Government learned that General Kornilov was planning an attempt to seize power for himself. In desperation, the Provisional Government decided it needed the well-organized Bolsheviks. It therefore released the Bolsheviks imprisoned in July and gave them guns to fight Kornilov.

Amongst the prisoners set free was Leon Trotsky. Although Trotsky had once been close to the Mensheviks, he was coming round more and more to Lenin's point of view. Now, he was elected Chairman of the Petrograd Soviet. Under his leadership, the Soviet organized its own small army, the Red Guard. It also formed the Military Revolutionary Committee which, he said, would defend Petrograd.

No wonder then that Lenin could hardly bear to be absent from the capital! On 30th September, he took the train to Vyborg just inside the Finnish frontier and only a few miles from Petrograd.

Above **The room in Helsinki where Lenin worked on his book** *The State and Revolution.*

"We must leave quite open the question of the length of time required for the withering away of the State, and the concrete forms it will take, since material for the solution of these questions is not available."
The State and Revolution, by Lenin.

15. The Leader

In Vyborg, Lenin felt much more in touch with the plans for the revolution. He was more and more convinced that the time for it had really come. Disguised with a wig and thick glasses, and without his beard, he was able to go to Petrograd for a very important meeting of the Central Committee of the Bolshevik Party on 25th October. It was held privately in the flat of one of the members. Lenin kept on repeating that "an armed uprising is inevitable and the time is fully ripe." Finally, he managed to convince most of the members present that this was true. Among the dissidents, to Lenin's dismay, was his great friend Zinoviev, as well as another loyal Bolshevik, Kameniev, who voted against this motion. They were afraid that another attempt at revolution would result in another failure, as had happened in July.

But events were moving too fast for differences of opinion of this sort to be very important. On 5th November the Provisional Government, for its part, decided to act. They ordered troops to break up the offices of the Bolshevik newspaper, *Rabochy Put* (*Workers' Path*). The telephone wires to the Bolshevik headquarters in the Smolny Convent (once an elegant girls' school) were cut. This was all the excuse Trotsky needed. He sent Bolshevik soldiers to defend the building. The revolution had begun.

"The Central Committee recognizes that the international situation of the Russian revolution ... also the the military situation ... also the fact that the proletarian parties have gained a majority in the Soviets – all this taken in conjunction with the peasant insurrection and the swing of popular confidence to our party [the elections in Moscow], finally the obvious preparation for a second Kornilov affair ... places the armed uprising on the order of the day.

"Recognizing, therefore, that an armed uprising is inevitable and that the time is fully ripe, the Central Committee proposes to all the party organizations to be guided accordingly, and to consider and decide all the practical questions ... from this point of view." *Lenin's secret proclamation, 24th October, 1917.*

Opposite **A detachment of Red Guards outside the Smolny Institute.**

Lenin, who always seemed to be away when matters came to a head, was back in hiding in Vyborg. He was just putting the finishing touches to yet another letter to his comrades in the capital, urging immediate revolt, when his landlady burst into his room with the news that the Provisional Government was seizing all the bridges, cutting off the heart of Petrograd from its suburbs. He could hardly wait until she had gone out again. He left a note for his wife: "I have gone where you did not want me to go," he wrote, "*au revoir, Ilyich.*" Then he snatched up his wig, tied a large white handkerchief round his face and set off. He hoped that if he were stopped by government guards they would think that he had tooth-ache. The way to Petrograd was fraught with danger for him. There were many government guards on the streets. If Lenin had been recognized, he would have been shot on sight.

But he managed to reach the Smolny Convent after only minor incidents. Once there, he had little difficulty in finding Trotsky's office, even though he had never been in Smolny before. Trotsky told him the news: a bloodless revolution was taking place. Detachments of Red Guards were leaving the Convent at regular intervals to take over the main points in Petrograd – like the railway stations and post offices. They were meeting no resistance.

Right through that night they talked, lying on the hard floor of the Smolny Convent, while the revolution swept silently through Petrograd.

By 8 o'clock the next morning there was little doubt that most of Petrograd was in Bolshevik hands. The only major point left was the Winter Palace where the Provisional Government was still sitting.

Lenin sat down that morning and drafted a proclamation to the people of Russia announcing the victory of the revolution. Power, he said, had passed into the

"History will not forgive revolutionaries for delays, when they could be victorious today (and will certainly be victorious today), while they risk losing much tomorrow, while they risk losing everything.

"If we seize power today, we seize it not against the Soviets but for them.

"Seizure of power is the basis of the uprising, its political purposes will be made clear after the seizure."
Lenin, 24th October, 1917.

Opposite **Grigory Zinoviev.**

71

hands of the Military Revolutionary Committee. He promised immediate peace-moves, the abolition of the landlords' ownership of the land, workers' control of industry, and the formation of a Soviet Government. The Military Revolutionary Committee published the proclamation at 10 o'clock and it was telegraphed from the captured radio station to all the provincial Soviets. It was printed on thousands of handbills which were scattered around the streets of Petrograd.

At two o'clock in the afternoon, the Petrograd Soviet met in the Smolny Convent. Trotsky, in a stirring speech from the platform, announced that the Provisional Government had been overthrown. He was very much the man of the moment. After all, it was Trotsky who had been behind the planning of the events of the past few weeks. Lenin, who spoke after him, sounded dull by comparison.

Lenin's big moment came in the evening. Smolny, still a hive of activity, was the scene of the opening of the Second Congress of Soviets. The victory of the revolution was again announced and, when they at last understood what this really meant, the moderate socialist members of the Soviets left the hall. They did not want to have anything more to do with the Bolsheviks. They would carry on their own fight elsewhere.

Lenin was left in the room with his own supporters. He seemed dazed with the wonder of the moment. He mounted the platform and told the Congress that it now possessed full powers and was the supreme ruler of Russia. As he sat down, the silence of the hall was shattered by applause. The delegates cheered. They threw their caps into the air. They shouted for Lenin. They sang the Internationale. By the end of the evening, Lenin was standing up too, singing with the rest, his eyes shining.

Next day, they were back in their chairs. Lenin, in

fact, had hardly slept. He had spent most of the night working out his plans for the following day. These plans were aimed at carrying out the promises he had made in his proclamation. He began with his Decree on Peace. This called for an end to the war which had caused the people suffering for such a long time. Once again, he was cheered. Once again, the Internationale was sung. Lenin stood on the platform, gripping the reading desk. His eyes travelled over his cheering audience. Someone who was there that day described him as a "short stocky figure, with a big head set down on his shoulders, bald and bulging, little eyes, a snubbish nose, wide, generous mouth, and heavy chin, clean-shaven now, but already beginning to bristle with the well-known beard of his past and future." But, at that moment, no-one cared that he looked odd and that his trousers seemed too long for him.

When the cheers had died down, Lenin announced his Decree on the Land. This proclaimed the end of private ownership of land except by simple peasants and simple Cossacks.

Lastly, the Congress discussed what it should call the members of its government. It did not like the title "minister," which it felt was too much connected with the old aristocratic figure of the diplomat. Trotsky's suggestion that they should be called "people's commissars" was finally accepted. Lenin was appointed President of the Soviet of People's Commissars.

The new leader of mighty Russia was taken home that night in a chauffeur-driven motor-car – an unusual phenomenon in the Russia of that period.

"The Provisional Government has been overthrown. State power has passed into the hands of the organ of the Petrograd Soviet, the Military Revolutionary Committee, which stands at the head of the Petrograd proletariat and garrison.

"The cause for which the people have been fighting – the immediate proposal of a democratic peace, the abolition of the landlords' ownership of land, workers' control over industry and the formation of a Soviet Government – this cause is assured.

"Long live the workers', soldiers' and peasants' revolution!" *Lenin's proclamation, October, 1917*

16. The Problems of Power

The first-ever President of the Soviet of People's Commissars settled down in an office in the Smolny Convent. He moved into a large corner room on the third floor and furnished it with the bare minimum of comforts. In fact, it contained nothing but an iron bed, a small table for his secretary, a desk for himself, three or four chairs and two wall telephones.

Russia at that particular moment was no easy country to govern. A large number of problems faced Lenin at this time. Three of them, however, were particularly urgent. Firstly, Alexander Kerensky, the former leader of the Provisional Government, had gathered together an army of Cossack soldiers and was leading a rebellion against the Bolsheviks. Lenin threw himself into organizing military defence. Quite soon, the unruly elements were subdued – at least for the time being.

The other two problems were less easily solved. It was absolutely necessary to hold elections for a people's parliament. A government which they could elect and which would represent their interests had always been one of the dearest dreams of the Russian people. But it was not one of Lenin's dreams. What if elections were held and the Bolsheviks did not poll the majority of votes? On the other hand, if he did not hold elections, how could he claim that he represented the workers and peasants of the country?

"It was very incautious of us not to have postponed it. But in the end it turned out for the best. The dispersal of the Constituent Assembly by the Soviet Government is a frank and complete liquidation of formal democracy in the name of the revolutionary dictatorship. It will be a good lesson."
Lenin to Trotsky. From Lenin, by Leon Trotsky.

Opposite **Lenin delivering a speech in Moscow, 1919.**

Right **A painting by the Soviet artist Brodsky,** *Lenin at Smolny.*

Lenin did his best to make sure that the Bolsheviks won the elections. He forbade political meetings by any other parties in the weeks beforehand. Yet, despite his efforts, the Bolshevik Party gained only a quarter of the total votes. Lenin was furious. He placed the Electoral Commission under arrest. He closed all the printing presses which produced leaflets for the other parties. He dissolved the Military Revolutionary Committee. In its place he put a new organization, the Cheka. The main aim of the Cheka was to terrorize all enemies of the regime into silence. But he could not prevent the new parliament, called the Constituent Assembly, from meeting.

However, he did not let it meet for long. The newly-elected members gathered on 18th January. Right from the start, every suggestion that the Bolsheviks made was rejected by the rest of the deputies. At last, all the Bolsheviks, led by Lenin, left the room. The meeting went on without them until the early hours of the next morning. Then Lenin ordered the lights in the hall to be turned out. The deputies were driven out at gun-point and Lenin declared the Constituent Assembly dissolved for ever.

He explained his action later by saying that it was the Soviets that had seized power in the revolution, not the Assembly. The Assembly, according to him, would merely have continued the policies of the Provisional Government.

The third problem that Lenin had to tackle in the first month after the revolution was how to bring about the peace he had promised. Russia was still, in theory, involved on the side of Britain and France in the war against Germany. Lenin had only one idea on this subject. He wanted to get Russia out of the war. If this meant agreeing to the very harsh peace conditions Germany was demanding, he was prepared to do so. He knew that Russia was too weak to go on fighting. Anyway, he expected the international socialist revolution to break out fairly soon which would unite the workers of every country.

Most of his comrades did not agree with him about signing the peace treaty on Germany's terms. They supported a plan Trotsky put forward. Trotsky's idea, which he put into practice, was to go along to the peace conference and announce that Russia would sign no peace treaty – she would simply withdraw from the war. Such a thing had never been heard of before! For a while the Germans did not know how to deal with such a situation. Then they found an easy solution – they said that unless Russia agreed to their peace terms, they would resume the war. Immediately, German troops went into action.

So, on 3rd March, 1918, Russia was forced to sign the treaty of Brest-Litovsk with Germany, accepting the terms she had refused before. By this treaty, she lost a quarter of her territory and nearly half her population.

"They tell you I will make a shameful peace. Yes. I will make a shameful peace. They tell you I will surrender Petrograd, the Imperial City. Yes. I will surrender Petrograd, the Imperial City. They tell you I will surrender Moscow, the Holy City. I will. I will go back to the Volga, and I will go back behind the Volga to Ekaterinburg; but I will save the soldiers of the revolution and I will save the revolution." *Lenin, 1918*

17. The Peace

The signing of the peace treaty at Brest-Litovsk did not bring peace to the land. No-one liked the terms of the treaty, neither the Russian people nor Russia's former allies, France and Britain. Both sides thought that Lenin had sold out to the Germans.

Lenin found himself surrounded by enemies in that spring of 1918. British and Japanese forces landed at Vladivostock. Kharkov was occupied by the Germans, who were now moving on to Odessa and the Crimea. The Czechs were attacking the Soviets on the Volga. Worst of all, many of his own Russian soldiers, sent home from the war when the peace was signed, had come back determined to overthrow the Soviet Government. Joined by many others who felt the same, they formed themselves into bands, called themselves the White Guards, and set out to win back their country. In these early days, the Bolshevik Red Guards were unable to hold them back.

The whole country was rent with war and famine, hunger and suffering. Lenin threw himself into the mammoth task of putting order into the chaos. With the Germans close to Petrograd, he had moved his government to Moscow. Here, he lived simply in one room in the Kremlin, the old home of the Russian Czars (he and Krupskaya even ate in the kitchen). It was from there that he determinedly pressed on with

"Workers and paupers, take a gun in your hands. Learn to shoot well. Be prepared for uprisings by Kulaks and White Guards. To the wall with all those who agitate against the Soviet power. Ten bullets for everyone who raises a hand against it.

"The bourgeoisie is an indefatigable enemy. The rule of capital will be extinguished only with the death of the last capitalist, the last landowner, priest and army officer."
From the Russian newspaper Pravda, August, 1918.

Opposite **Japanese occupation units at Vladivostock, 1918.**

Above **Russian revolutionaries being hanged by German-Austrian occupying forces during their occupation of the Ukraine, 1918.**

"In principle we have never renounced, and cannot renounce terrorism . . . It is an act of war, indispensable at a certain point in the struggle." *Lenin, writing in Iskra, 1901.*

his policy. He engaged specialists to deal with economic re-organization and paid them very high salaries. On the other hand, he took property away from the Kulaks, the rich peasants. He put all workers under strict military discipline and people who did not work properly were very severely punished. Any newspapers which criticized the Bolsheviks were banned.

All these measures made people dislike the Bolsheviks more and more. Lenin found that the only way he could get his decrees obeyed was by using force. Punishments inflicted on those who disobeyed him became harsher and harsher.

How he had changed in these months! He no longer believed that he could bring people round to his ideas by arguing with them and persuading them. Now he felt that force was the only way. Words were a waste of time, only violence was of any use. ". . . Remember that the Lenin who talked to you ten years ago no longer has any existence," he told a friend at this time. "He died a long time ago. In his place there speaks the new Lenin . . ." He summed up the reason for the change in his personality when he said to Trotsky: "You know, from persecution and living illegally to come suddenly into power, it's too rough altogether."

As the government used more and more violence, those who were against it did the same. Already, shortly before the meeting of the Constituent Assembly, someone had tried to kill Lenin. At roughly the same period, two former Provisional Government ministers were killed when they were ill in hospital. No action was taken against the murderer. His action was condoned as an act of "political terror." In these months, one murder followed another. On 6th July, 1918, the German envoy to the Kremlin was the victim. On this occasion too, the real assassin went free, and the government punished hundreds of innocent social revolutionaries whom it said were responsible. On 16th July, 1918, Czar Nicholas II and all his household (children and servants included) were shot in the house they had been staying in in Ekaterinburg at the order of the local Bolsheviks. On 30th August, 1918, Uritsky, chairman of the Petrograd Cheka, was assassinated. Matters reached a ghastly climax on the evening of that same day. Lenin had addressed a workers' meeting at the Corn Exchange in the Basmannaya district of Moscow. As he was leaving, shots rang out. Lenin fell to the ground, with one bullet in his neck and another in his shoulder.

"It was in those tragic days that something snapped in the heart of the revolution. It began to lose its 'kindness' and 'forbearance'." *Lenin, by Leon Trotsky.*

Below **Czar Nicholas II in captivity at Czarskoe-Selo, late 1917.**

81

F

18. "Order, Discipline, Organization"

The attempt on Lenin's life was followed by a fresh bout of terror. The Petrograd Cheka alone executed over eight hundred "enemies of the people" in revenge.

Lenin himself recovered quickly from his wounds. Krupskaya's loving nursing helped considerably. His own iron will did the rest. He was back at his desk in just over a fortnight.

There was certainly work for him to do. The last months of 1918 and all of 1919 was not a happy period for Russia. The end of the Great War on 11th November, 1918, had added to the problems facing the country. In the first place, British and French troops were no longer needed to fight Germany. Instead, they were sent to strengthen the White Army in its fight against the Bolsheviks. The Red Army was suffering defeat after defeat. Secondly, British and French ships were blockading Russian ports, stopping goods from abroad coming in. Factories could not get raw materials to work with, many had closed down completely, and others were operating at a fraction of their normal capacity. In addition, there was a severe shortage of skilled workers. Economic activity in the country had almost come to a halt. War had been followed by famine and famine had caused an epidemic of a terrible disease, typhus. Thousands of people were dying.

These problems made Lenin think again about some

Above **Lenin walking in the Kremlin yard after recovering from his wounds, October, 1918.**

Opposite **Red Army recruits.**

83

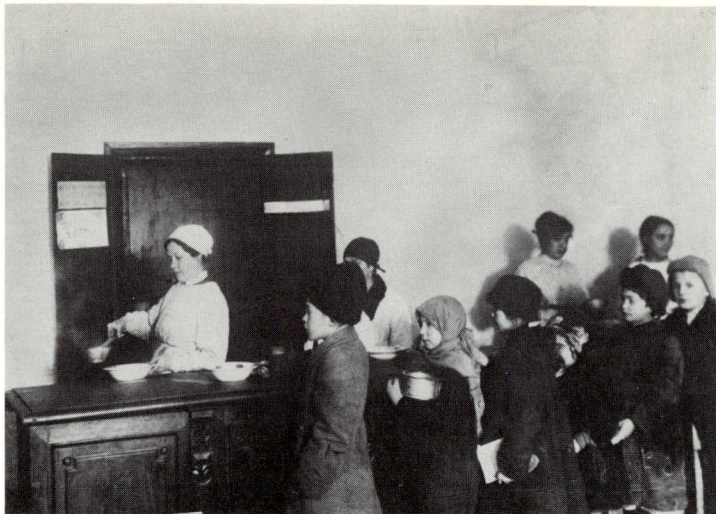

Right **Children of Petrograd being given food during a famine in 1918.**

of his basic Marxist ideas. Was the Russian worker competent to take over the government of the country? Was it possible for the state to wither away, as he had once thought? Was government not the business of experts? As he questioned his faith in the Russian worker, Lenin put a new faith in technology. "Communism is Soviet power plus the electrification of the whole country," he said somewhere around this time. "Order, discipline, organization" became the new catchwords of the party.

Trotsky put these ideas into force when he reorganized the Red Army. After the revolution officers had been elected by the ordinary soldiers, according to good socialist principles. Now, Trotsky brought back the old professional officers who had led the Czar's armies. He controlled this "new" army with an iron hand and very strict discipline. He went tearing up and down the battle front in an armoured train to make sure that his orders were being obeyed. Gradually, the tide turned in favour of the Bolshevik forces. Defeat

"Socialism . . . is nothing else but a monopoly of state capitalism instituted for the benefit of the whole nation, and by virtue of that ceasing to be a capitalist monopoly." *Lenin, Works.*

84

turned to victory. In 1920, the Red Army re-captured the Crimea. The Civil War was officially over. "Order, discipline and organization" had triumphed.

Lenin first tried to tackle the economic problem with terror. He accused hundreds of administrators, technicians and skilled workers of "economic sabotage" and had them shot. He sent food detachments to the countryside to take grain from the peasants by force if they refused to give up their surplus production of their own free will. These measures only made things worse. Production continued to drop.

It was then that Lenin had to recognize fully that the Russian worker would not work properly unless he had the prospect of making a profit from it. He was not prepared to give of his best purely to serve the revolution. With this in mind, Lenin introduced his New Economic Policy (known as N.E.P.) in 1921. This put some of the features of the once-hated capitalism into Soviet socialism. Before, selling for profit had been a crime, now it was encouraged. Farmers were allowed to sell their grain on the open market for their own profit instead of giving it up to the state. Small industries could now be run by private individuals instead of the state. Different rates of wages were offered in factories to encourage employees to work better. And it paid off. Almost immediately, Russia's production began to rise.

At the same time as granting this new economic freedom, Lenin tightened up on political discipline. Before, he had said that the right to criticize was "the duty of the revolutionary." Now all criticism of the party was forbidden. The revolutionary's only duty was to obey. Lenin told the Cheka to deal with political disobedience "strictly, severely and mercilessly."

"It was a fantastic idea for a Communist to dream that in three years you could drastically change the economic structure of our country . . . and let us confess our sins: there were many such fantasy-makers in our midst. But how can you begin a Socialist revolution in our country without fantasy-makers?" *Lenin at the Tenth Congress, 1921.*

"We have sinned . . . in going too far in nationalizing trade and industry, in closing down local commerce. Was this a mistake? Undoubtedly." *Lenin introducing N.E.P. in 1921.*

19. Death of a Dictator

In the spring of 1921, drought, dust-storms and locusts ruined the harvest in the rich farming lands round the River Volga. Famine followed. The starving peasants left their farms and came to the cities. Thousands, tens of thousands died of starvation. The situation was so appalling, the death rate so high, that Lenin was forced to accept help from capitalist countries abroad. The American Red Cross and other American relief organizations moved in, bringing assistance.

Lenin had other worries in these years. His health was failing. He was suffering from blinding head-aches. He was also becoming more and more worried about the vast numbers of Communist officials. They were turning into a large privileged class of their own. They were not even efficient: quite the reverse. He tackled this last problem at the eleventh congress of the Communist Party, in March, 1922. White and drawn, he recommended that a new post be set up, that of General Secretary to the Central Committee of the Communist Party, as a means of making government more efficient. To fill this post he chose quite a minor commissar, a man called Joseph Stalin. Lenin thought that Stalin was the right man for the job because he was ambitious and worked hard.

He could not do anything about his terrible head-aches. We can guess how much they troubled him from

Above **Famine victims in their hovel at Samara Camp, October, 1921.**

Opposite **Lenin with his wife in 1922.**

87

Above **Lenin with Joseph Stalin, 1922.**

the fact that he asked Trotsky to be deputy chairman of the Soviet at this time. This was more or less the same thing as naming Trotsky as his successor. But Trotsky refused. He knew he was not as brilliant as Lenin and felt unworthy of the job. He did not want to create the jealousy that being known as Lenin's heir would arouse. And he did not get on with Stalin. If he accepted he was afraid that he would split the party.

In May, 1922, Lenin had a stroke. He was desperately ill. Not until the autumn was he able to return to work in Moscow. He was horrified to find that while he had been away, Stalin had been carefully taking greater and greater power into his own hands. He realized that he did not have much time left to put things right. In December, he had a second stroke. Painfully, he dictated a statement. In it, he urged that the Communist Central Committee be made very much larger. It should contain many more representatives of the workers. He was becoming more and more afraid of Stalin's ambition and the violence of his methods. Such a man, he felt, could not be trusted with the dictatorship of the country. He also suffered feelings of guilt about the dictatorship he himself had practised over the workers. "I am, I believe, strongly guilty before the workers of Russia . . ." he wrote at that time.

Lenin was laid low by a third stroke when the twelfth Congress was held in January, 1923. Trotsky too was ill, though not so seriously, and tied to his bed. With the two great leaders absent, the way was clear for Stalin. He took advantage of the opportunity. By the time the Congress closed, he was on his way to becoming undisputed leader of Russia.

On 21st January, 1923, Lenin died. Two days later, his body, lying in an uncovered coffin, was carried by train from his estate in Gorki to Moscow. The twenty-mile route was lined with crowds of weeping people, "orphaned," as Zinoviev later said. The father of the revolution had gone.

Above **Lenin in a wheelchair during his last illness.**

"Lenin lives on in the heart of every good workman,
"Lenin lives on in the heart of every poor peasant,
"Lenin lives on in the millions of colonial slaves,
"Lenin lives on in the camp of our enemies, in the hate they have for Leninism, Communism and Bolshevism."
Funeral proclamation on the day of Lenin's death.

Principal Characters

Axelrod, Paul (1850–1928). An exiled Marxist leader living in Zurich.

Bronstein, Leon Davydovitch (known as Trotsky) (1879–1940). Prominent revolutionary and writer. Author of one of the best histories of the revolution.

Gorki, Maxim (1868–1936). Revolutionary writer.

Kerensky, Alexander Fyodorovich (1881–1970). Liberal politician, head of the Provisional Government for most of its existence.

Kornilov, General Georgievich (1870–1918). Right-wing general under the Provisional Government.

Martov, Julius (1873–1923). Revolutionary friend of Lenin's who later broke with him.

Plekhanov, Georgy Valentinovich (1857–1918). An exiled Marxist leader living in Geneva.

Potresov, Alexander (1869–1934). Editor of *Iskra* with Lenin and Martov.

Stalin, Joseph (1879–1953). Minor commissar who became the dictator of Soviet Russia in the 1920s. Instituted the First Five Year Plan in 1928.

Ulyanov, Alexander (Sasha) (1866–1887). Lenin's brother.

Ulyanov, Maria Alexandrovna (1837–1916). Lenin's mother.

Zinoviev, Grigory Evseyevich (1883–1936). Prominent revolutionary, friend of Lenin.

Table of Dates

1870   Vladimir Ilyich Ulyanov (Lenin) born

1887   Alexander Ulyanov (Sasha) hanged

1891   Lenin qualifies as a lawyer

1895   Lenin arrested and imprisoned

1897   Lenin exiled to Siberia

1898   First Congress of the Russian Social Democratic Party in Minsk

1898   Lenin marries Nadezhda Krupskaya

1900   Lenin leaves Siberia for European Russia

1900   First issue of *Iskra*

1902   *What is to be Done?* published

1903   Lenin resigns from *Iskra*

1904   Outbreak of Russo-Japanese war

1905   First issue of *Vperyod* published. Bloody Sunday. Lenin returns to St. Petersburg from Switzerland. The Czar publishes his October Manifesto.

1906   Elections to the Duma

1914   Great War declared

1917   February Revolution begins. Lenin leaves Switzerland in sealed train. Bolshevik party decides on immediate revolution. Provisional Government raids Bolshevik offices; the revolution begins

1918   The Constituent Assembly meets for the first and last time. Treaty of Brest-Litovsk signed. Great War ends

1921   New Economic Policy officially announced
1922   Lenin's first stroke
1924   Lenin dies

N.B. All these dates are according to the "new style" European calendar. Until February, 1918, Russia actually used an old and different form of dating.

Further Reading

Kochan, Lionel. *Russia in Revolution* (Paladin, 1971). A straightforward description of the events of the revolution set in their historical background.

Payne, Robert. *The Life and Death of Lenin* (Pan Books, 1964). A detailed biography of Lenin but very easy to read, with lots of quotations from the diaries, letters and anecdotes of the people concerned.

Reed, John. *Ten Days that Shook the World* (Random House, New York, 1960). A vivid account of the November Revolution by an American journalist who witnessed it.

Trotsky, Leon. *On Lenin* (Harraps, 1971). Notes made by Trotsky for a biography of Lenin, which throws a great deal of light on the character of both men.

Ulam, Adam. *Lenin and the Bolsheviks* (Fontana Books, 1969). Concentrates more on Lenin as a politician and on the rise of the Bolsheviks. For older age group.

Index

Picture Credits

The author and publishers wish to thank all those who have given permission for the reproduction of copyright illustrations on the following pages: Radio Times Hulton Picture Library, 34, 36, 40, 46, 47, 56, 62, 66, 68, 70, 81, 87, 89; Popperfoto, 10, 28, 76, 86; Illustrated London News, 11; Novosti Press Agency, *frontispiece*, 8, 9, 12, 13, 14, 16, 18, 19, 20, 22, 23, 24, 27, 30, 31, 32, 35, 38, 42, 43, 44, 48, 50, 51, 52, 54, 58, 60–61, 64, 65, 67, 74, 78, 80, 82, 83, 84.